Voices Through The Midnight Mist

Of candles, vanilla pages and misty moors...

Oindrilla Das

BookLeaf Publishing

India | USA | UK

Made with ❤ on the BookLeaf Publishing Platform
www.bookleafpub.in
www.bookleafpub.com

Dedication

To the bridge of hearts,

who converts discord to harmony,

and darkness to light.

Your wisdom, patience, and benevolence

have healed that which was broken,

and for this, this book finds its soul in you.

With heartfelt gratitude, I dedicate these verses to you—

a true mediator, a word-healer, and a keeper of peace.

Preface

Love has always been our greatest storyteller. It
whispers and roars, silences that echo years and words
that change the direction of hearts. Voices Through the
Midnight Mist is a coming together of
love's countless voices—some longing, some fulfilled,
some standing on the edge of the unknown.

Midnight is a border, an hour of crossing
where the dream and the reality entwine,
where confessions are breathed under moonlight and
memories are deposited like the fog on lonely streets. It
is in such fragile, airy hours that love is most stripped,
unpresented, open and unguarded.

This anthology gathers voices
from across love's endless world—poets,
writers, dreamers who have lived it in fleeting poems,
heartbreak tales, and quiet epiphanies. Each piece is
a beacon in the mist, illuminating the longing, passion,
and tenderness that unite us beyond space and time.

Let these words echo in you, let you hear the echoes of
your own heart within them, and let love, in all

its infinite variations, continue to guide you through
the fog.

Acknowledgements

This book would not have been possible without the support and love of a lot of people. However, one person particularly stands out for going out of his way to repair what had once been broken and bring back what had once been lost. Thank you for enabling me to write once more by brushing aside my inhibitions and tending to every wound. To you, I owe you this work...

1. In Silence...

It is in the silence that I remember you,
Softly whispering in my ear,
Like the rustling of leaves on a cold winter night,
The stories of a bygone year.

It is in the silence that I remember you,
By the fireplace crackling through the night,
The glow of its embers wrap me warm,
Like the blanket of your eyes.

It is in the silence that I remember you,
Whilst the snow piles up my sill,
The last leaf strains against the branches, white,
And I wonder, do you remember me still?

2. The Night of the Highwayman

He came riding through the moors that night,
The mist swirling in his wake,
Whilst the silver moon hid herself,
To aid him on his way.

He was the shadow of the starless night,
His cloak billowing in the wind,
A candlelight his only goal
A lone message on a window-sill.

He rode the night, swift as the wind,
His horse a blur of snow,
And whilst the stream gurgled by,
He begged the night to grow.

For through the mist he saw the light,
That beckoned him from afar,
Placed solely for his eyes alone,
A rendezvous in the dark.

She watched the night with bated breath,
The silver stream snaking through,
When through the silence she heard a sound
The soft pad of galloping hooves.

She waited in silent stealth,
Her candle flickering in the wind.
As he rode in through the misty night,
to stand beneath her 'sill.

A softened glance,
A hidden smile,
Eyes they twinkle bright,
A warm embrace
A hidden kiss,
Lovers of the night.

Too soon the moon set over the moor
Too soon the hues of day
Too soon 'twas time to be apart.
To ride into the gray.

Till another night when the misty moor,
Basks 'neath the moonlit sky,
The candle shall flare,

Through cold winter days,
Till the highwayman rides by.

4

3. Once Again...

The night was a blur of lights and sounds,
Of laughter drifting to my ears,
The clink of glasses and a hidden smile,
Memories of bygone years.

We have had our falls, our toils and snares,
Our dances in the rain
The hidden glances, the whispered thoughts
Flit through my mind again.

The gleam in your eye breaks into a smile
As Time stands still once more,
Beneath the trees that blossomed in pink,
Two souls meet from long ago.

4. Behind the Lines...

By the river of my motherland
We walked in silence, hand in hand.
The winds of change blew through our hair
The day was fine, the day was fair.
With you by my side we walked,
Neither speaking, but deep in thought.
For sadness filled your heart and mine,
Woe! The tricks played by Father Time.

Were we not promised a future bright?
To just end in blood and fight!

The bugle call stops your tread
Your heart, I know, fills with dread.
Your hand it feels so cold on mine,
My heart it aches to stop the time.
But this cruel world, it waits for none,
For you to leave, the time has come.
You turn back once for me to see,
That long loved face I yearn to feel.

The bugle calls one more time,
You ride away, I'm left behind.

Days and nights they melt in one,
Eyes that search, but find no one.
The sun it shines but fails to warm
The icy fear that fills my heart.

Will the day you come arrive?
In hope and trust, each day I survive

With hope in my heart I live through the day,
Ignoring the news of death and decay.
At church the wails of mothers I hear,
And\my heart, my heart, it numbs with fear.
The day you came, it came at last,
With four men and a wooden cask..!

5. Our Park Once More...

I walked by our park again,
Our bench by the glistening lake,
The flowers of spring are blooming still,
To be swept by the brush of a rake.

I walked by our park again,
Memories they come floating by,
Of laughter and frolic of mundane days,
Time that swiftly swept by.

I walked by our park again,
My bare feet on the grass,
The sun sets in a golden glow,
Like freshly sanded glass.

I walked by our park again,
And laid down 'neath the trees,
The flowers swaying in the breeze,
Dreams of you and me.

6. Raas Leela...

It began on a warm winter's day,
Really strange for the time.
I should have known that very morn,
The bell for change had chimed.

I watched as you climbed those polished stairs,
The wood creaking 'neath your feet,
Heart fluttering as you went by,
And I slowly took my seat.

The crowd they gasped in mocking wonder,
As gently you took the stage,
How could a boy of golden splendor,
Spin on spot with grace?

You faced the crowd with a nervous smile,
The shock in their eyes and hearts,
And steeled yourself to break the walls,
Of age-old rules and tasks.

The Gods must have opened the Heavens that day,
As wood to anklet was heard,
As you danced to the beat of a million dreams,
That shattered before they stirred.

And then you took your flute to hand,
Dancing to the tunes of lore,
And all at once in each heart stirred
A story from long ago.

Soon in you they saw the Truth,
So hidden in their Time.
And blinds of prejudice fell apart at seams,
Through dance of light they shined.

7. The Masks Have Fallen...

I heard you were asking about me,
In whispers to your friend...
The memories of a past flit through your mind...
And your heart it fills with regret.

You placed your trust in the wrong
And pushed the dear ones aside
And now when the masks have fallen apart
In tears and pain you reside.

I walked away some time ago,
In silence I waited to see
Your world soon unravelling into threads
Reality a misery.

Yet I never once turned away,
But build the walls I broke,
To protect what was left of me
From the pain from long ago.

Yet now you ask for me once more,
And the pain it rushes through
The cracks I did not know exists
In the walls I built against you.

It seems my heart never forgot the times
When it grew fond of your smile
It bleeds still red when you're in pain
Oh! so naïve this heart of mine.

8. The Hidden Door...

The door still remains open in the wall,
The vines growing steady 'neath its shade,
The flowers have long shed their fragrance to the world,
But the birds still stand in wait.

The door still creaks when pushed to the side,
The garden still in disarray,
The grass now high like oaks in the night,
Of a full moon in the month of May.

It waits in silence as the days pass on,
Wondering about the trysts at night,
Of two gentle souls rambling on the shores
Lovers 'neath the moonlight.

Soon they would part
As the day it broke,
The Sun awakening with a yawn,
Whilst the trees would wait for the two hearts again;
To finally become one.

Yet days had passed
Since last they had part,
And the flowers had shed their hue,
In terrible fear,
That the end was near,
For the forbidden love so soon.

With hope in their hearts,
They waited in line,
To watch the old wooden door,
Till finally it creaked
And they swayed in glee,
As the ring on her finger shone.

The two sat down,
'Neath the blanket of Stars,
And the breeze rustled through the leaves,
And the moon it danced to the cricket's buzz,
Love blossoming 'neath the trees.

9. The Window...

It was my favourite spot,
My window,
It looked out to a park,
A huge oak tree from whence the leaves
Flitted to the ground.

I watched the changing colours,
Of the flowers that lined the grove,
The final fall of the last leaf gone,
Branches struggling through the snow.

With coffee in hand and a book on my lap,
I watched the seasons storm by,
The years march on to the beat of the drums
As silence falls with a 'sigh'.

I turn my book, the pages white,
Yet read I none the words,
The vanilla scent flits softly by,
As I look for the half healed hurt.

The rose it peeps through the pages soft
Black as the starless night,
The soft scent of love
Long gone and lost,
To the vagaries of Time.

It was my favourite spot,
My window,
It looked out to a park,
A huge oak tree still in view,
Just you not in my arms.

10. Meant to Be...

Maybe we were not meant to be,
Destined to drift apart,
To the storms of time and words of vice,
To be doomed from the start.

Yet your memories and your laugh,
Guide me through the day,
The sweet joy of remembrance,
Pushing me along the way.

There's not a day that passes by,
When I don't hear your voice,
Calming the tempest in my mind,
Trying to move on.

Maybe we were not meant to be,
Destined to drift apart,
But there's not another I could love as much,
With you resides my heart.

11. A Little Too Much...

She won't cry,
But if you look into her eyes,
You'll see a girl
Who drives a little too fast,
Who laughs a little too hard,
Who smiles a little too long,
Who seems a little too strong.

Someone who keeps a little too busy
Someone who is always where you need her to be,
Someone who paints a little too dark,
Someone who is the party's spark.

Someone whose smiles don't reach her eyes,
Someone who laughs when her heart it cries,
Someone who won't let her pain seep through,
The walls that she built strongly around you.

Someone you think has moved on,
Someone who still dreams about your call,

Someone if once you look into her eyes,
Will drown in love that still resides.

She won't cry, her tears have dried..
Her care for you too strong...,
But her eyes, her eyes, like embers at night...
The love or you still burns.

12. The Book...

I've been hiding my tears for long,
I won't cry again,
The open book that I was to you,
Lies, tattered, misused and stained.

I've wrapped it up with velvet threads,
Bound it with a golden noose,
The emblem now of glittering ember,
Fixed just where the heart was used.

For the world and you now,
My book looks elegant and naive,
To be stored with absolute care,
In the midst of a library find.

Only when one is able to pierce the lock
And turn it's covers again,
Will they be able to see the pages inside,
Long forlorn, lost and stained.

So I've covered my broken book for you,
Taken the key away for good,
No need to see the damage been left behind
Let the pages be hidden from you.

13. The Night the Sky Burst...

The sky it burst,
As the world it slept,
'neath the obsidian clouds,
Till the lightning flashed,
And the thunder roared,
Her time on Earth had come.

She descended from the heavens,
Ethereal maiden,
Silver anklets at her feet,
The stage all set
To welcome her next,
And for her to dance with glee.

The curtains they lift,
And the beats burst forth,
She garbed in mist and hail,
Her dance of joy,
On parched dry soil,

Leaving rivulets in her trail.

She dances in tune,
To the Heavenly drums,
Her skirt flows in waves of light,
While the earth it soaks
In the soothing show,
And breathes in great respite.

I wake up to hear
Her anklets trilling,
Beat against my frosty pane,
The city lights glitter
To her pitter-patter,
As I witness the dance of the Rain.

14. Remember me...

When you remember me once again,
Look for me in the wilderness,
Where the wind blows wild,
And the flowers grow untamed...

When you remember me again,
Look for me 'neath the moon,
Where the elves play through the night,
And the fireflies feed on dew.

When you remember me again,
Look for me in the rain,
That quenches the parched earth,
And disappears in her embrace.

When you remember me once again,
Search for me once more,
I'll be waiting 'neath the stars so bright,
In our meadow from long ago.

15. Innocent Dreams...

There was a time
Not so long ago,
When the skies were blue,
Streets filled with snow.

Cherry blossoms
Lined the streets,
Sweet fragrance filled
For you and me.

The lake had frozen,
The bears at rest,
The sound of silence,
Put to test,
By the giggling girls
On sheets of ice,
Skating in circles,
In pure delight

We watched them turn,

Fairies in the snow,
Arms spread out
Like wings of gold.

They twirled and danced,
To strings of wind,
Blowing through the trembling
Of swiftly falling leaves.

We watched as the day
It turned to night
The snow sparkling clear
In the pale moon light.
The fairies they glistened,
As they danced to and fro
Till dropped they down
To the cold iced floor.

They laughed in glee,
Shattering through the night,
As the stars they paled,
To the glow of the flies.

We watched them long
For a little while more,
Reveling in innocence,
That was lost long ago.

We went on our way,
A path of shattered dreams,
Leaving the ice
To melt into spring.

Perhaps the fairies
They too had to grow,
Their innocence left behind,
To be seen never more.
Yet, the moment still remains,
Etched in my mind,
A moment of pure joy.
Amidst amber fireflies.

16. Eyes...

The eyes they never lie they say,
Mysterious as the depths of oceans,
Souls shining through the darkest night,
A myriad of unspoken emotions.

You told me you, didn't wait for me,
Memories slipping like sand through years,
Yet when I see you now again,
Your eyes they fill with tears...

We pause a while and the years roll back,
The wrinkles fade 'neath your eyes,
And once again we're back 'neath the stars
With you right in my arms.

So we stop a while and go our way
For we weren't meant to be
Yet in our thoughts and in our minds
Your heart still lies with me.

17. Neverland...

A thousand souls entwined as one,
A thousand voices soar,
A thousand hearts beat to the sound,
Of the wind that slowly blows.

We watch as the girls dressed in white,
March on fields of gold
With azure belts and silver crowns,
Pearls on lattice sown.

The watch no one,
One with the earth,
As the clouds start rolling in,
And dance they now
With ribbons white,
Around the pole that slowly spins.

They sing a song
Lost to the world,
The tune seeps like glistening sand

And lulling sleep
Soft and deep
Mist of Neverland.

18. Snow Queen...

The moon was in full tonight,
The stars had gone to rest,
The river a silver ribbon wide,
Etching the world in grey.

I walked through the trees of night,
The light filtering through the leaves,
The flitting of fireflies in the dark,
Reality slipping through a sieve.

The soft carpet of moss and dew,
The fragrance in the air,
Lingers in every finger tip,
That touches the autumn air.

I walk on feet of winter white,
My skirt edged with snow,
The flowers shiver in my stead,
And the leaves bow down to the floor.

The canopy shall soon be bare,
The moss sleeping under frost
When I release my wintry breath,
Till the autumn wind is lost.

My crown it glistens in the dark,
Like diamonds in the sky,
Eyes of grey, silver flecked,
I wear my winter smile.

19. Bury me Alive...

Bury me alive
Bury me deep
I shall soon bloom and grow
For I am a seed.

I thrive in darkness,
Moist in the soil,
My roots my anchor,
To serve my toils.

Rip me apart,
Push me deep,
I'll soon break through,
For I am a seed.

Mighty shall I grow,
Taller than the sky,
Your axes mere scratches,
On my armour so fine.

I'll shade those who care,
And bear fruit for those in need,
But never shall it fall again,
Hyperion resides in me.

20. The Walk...

Today I watched a miracle,
A change in the world that was:
A world filled with barriers,
For those that fight for a cause

A world of misogynies,
A world of strife,
A world of patriarchy,
A world.meang to hide.

She was told she could never be,
Her life within the walls,
Meant to live by the rules,
Never to aim for it all.

Yet she walked out into the field,
Her head held high,
"A gentleman's game", they said.
Let a woman try.

She did not let the calls,
Deter her in her stride.
Her bat speaking words,
With every cover drive.

And when she left the pitch,
To take her final stand
Ten thousand stood on their feet,
In reverence calpped their hands.

That day the night stood still in awe
And the world at her feet
And in the floodlight of her walk
For change she planted the seed.

21. Lady of Mist and Moon...

The world was a pool of mist that night,
The time I saw her last,
Her cloak of emerald green and grey
Billowing in the dark.

She watched me from her horse of white,
Her eyes a sea of storms,
And in silence she waited with bated breath,
For my inconsiderate response.

Her heart I tore apart that night,
And yet she shed no tear,
But in her eyes I saw the light,
Of longing disappear.

She said no word and turned her mare,
And rode into the mist,
The moon now hiding in the clouds,
She never to be seen.

I hear she rides alone at night,
Companion of the moon,
Her heart locked and iron clad,
She yearns for.the end too soon.

We were not meant to be,
Yet I long to wrap her in arms,
How do I tell her the truth,
That she has always had my heart.

I ride with her in my dreams of night
From dawn, to dusk, to noon,
My one true love, with eyes of storm,
My Lady of Mist and Moon.

22. Helen

The sun glittered through the leaves that day,
Pouring in showers of gold,
Whilst the daffodils swayed in the evening breeze,
To the smiles of young and old.

There on the banks she lay in white,
Her hair a blanket of gold,
Eyes closed in sweet reverie,
Beauty in tales be told.

She let the sun warm her skin,
The glow burnished in brown,
They saw, she knew, only her beauty to view,
The battle scars hidden 'neath her gown.

For whence has a dame been immortalised in words
If not for beauty alone?
The scars of battle to be hidden by smoke,
To be forgotten in memories and lore.